You Can Never Speak Up Too Often
For the Love of All Things

by

Paul R. Fleischman, M.D.

PARIYATTI PRESS

867 LARMON RD
ONALASKA, WA 98570, USA
WWW.PARIYATTI.COM

ISBN 1-928706-10-X

Library of Congress Control Number: 2001036117

Cover photograph by Forrest D. Fleischman; ©2004, Forrest D. Fleischman

Printed on 100% recycled New Leaf Opaque 70# Text

DISTRIBUTED BY INDEPENDENT PUBLISHERS GROUP

CONTENTS

Peru

At Home

For S.

When, in disgrace with fortune and men's eyes,

I all alone beweep my outcast state,

And trouble deaf heaven with my bootless cries,

And look upon myself, and curse my fate,

Wishing me like to one more rich in hope,

Featured like him, like him with friends possess'd,

Desiring this man's art and that man's scope,

With what I most enjoy contented least;

Yet in these thoughts myself almost despising,

Haply I think on thee, and then my state,

Like to the lark at break of day arising

From sullen earth, sings hymns at heaven's gate;

     For thy sweet love remember'd such wealth brings

     That then I scorn to change my state with kings.

— William Shakespeare, Sonnet 29

. . . wherever anyone may be imprisoned,

wherever anyone is made to suffer in the dying year,

I will be there, whispering in the ceaseless tides.

I will drift through open windows,

and, hearing me, eyes will glance upward

saying, How can we get to the ocean?

And, without answering, I will pass on

the collapse of foam and liquid sand . . .

the gray keening of birds on the shore. . .

And so, through me, freedom and the sea

will bring solace to the downcast heart.

—Pablo Neruda, from "The Poet's Task,"

(Translated from the Spanish by Alfred Corn)

Introduction

Poetry has always been accorded higher communicative authority than prose because poetry is intrinsically inspired. Poetry means charged language, and is the medium for scripture: Bible, Koran, Gita, or Sutta.

The Buddha frequently burst into song or poetry. Sometimes he delivered entire *suttas*, or discourses, in verse, and he also concluded prose *suttas* with poems. Apparently he felt that rhythmic and imagistic language were often the best vehicles to convey the spirit of his teaching.

The person from whom I have learned meditation for a quarter of a century, Mr. S. N. Goenka, has peppered his own prose discourses with verses quoted from the Buddha in the original Pāli language; and he has written his own explanatory Hindi poetry, through which he has enriched his logical descriptions with more ebullient expression. Some aspects of meditation instruction actually require the vibration of poetry in order to be conveyed, for only via poetry can the language transmit the love or joy that is signified. Fully expressed by either the Buddha or by Mr. Goenka, meditation travels along a particular vibrato.

In the poems collected here, you will find themes from the world of meditation. They are based upon personal experience in a variegated modern matrix. The poems contain no meditation instruction nor explanation, but their inspiration is this: to promote loving kindness in a world of kinship through realization of impermanence.

I have tried to return to classical poetry that rests on ideas and clear positions, and then amplifies them with images, suggestions, evocations, descriptions, perceptions, metaphors, parables—inner and outer life. Social and ethical values are emphatically present. But the poetry is predominantly the outpouring of a good year or two of mature life overflowing into thoughts, phrases, rhythms, repetitions, pauses, pictures, informative and devotional experiences.

I have attempted to reproduce on the page the soft and shifting rhythms of speech through free verse that can be put out quietly and directly into a microphone of a library or lecture hall, or into a room of friends, avoiding jingling or fancy ornamentation, clearly understandable to a listener who has no text to follow. The poems are personal statements of a jet-aged, interconnected, professional and private, contemplative and active life translated into organically rhythmic American English.

I have tried to integrate complex biological and scientific thought with poetic and reverential apprehension.

I have tried to capture the red or lunar poignance that the realization of impermanence brings to the phenomenal world of beings in this plane which mingles suffering with joyful inklings of liberation.

Amherst, Massachusetts
October, 2000

You Can Never Speak Up Too Often
For the Love of All Things

Sweet Pond, Guilford, Vermont, May 31, 1999—Memorial Day

You can never speak up too often for the love of all things.
For every living thing or natural place on earth, there is someone
        who wants to kill or destroy it;
Therefore, you can never speak up too often for the love of all things.

These families of geese that I watch as I sit beside the pond,
Two pairs, four adults, with their clutches of downy goslings
        who are carefully sheltered between the
        tall-necked, attendant goose and gander,
There is a hunter who yearns to kill them,
Who feels entitled to his killing of them,
Who would be outraged if you implied he had no right to
        gun them down in season.

This pond, set like an opal in the precious ring of earth,
        windsparkling among shaded forests of hemlock and pine,
There is someone waiting to race his motorboat across it,
        knifing the soft skin of its silence,
        leaking oil into its pearl waters;
        develop it, build beaches,

bring in crowds with boomboxes surging across
        macadamized parking lots;
Therefore, you can never speak up too often for the love of all things.

All beings spring up from the same womb of life.
Sunlight strikes the earth, plants catch it, and as they hold light
        in their secret birthing place,
The embryo of life unfolds in their leaves and seeds.
This green gift of light becomes the food that feeds
        the worlds of birds and beasts and men.
All beings share the same joy that flows in the company of other lives.
All beings share the same tremor in the face of death.
Therefore, you can never speak up too often with the love of all things.

The silence found throughout the world in evening ponds,
        unbroken forests, mountain-enfolded ravines,
        hilltops at dusk,
Is not an absence of noise, but a presence.
In the company of silence, people hear more clearly the passage of eternity,
        rustling between the lattice of the cells of their own mind,
        like wind through a screen.
In the calm of silence—as if its arms were folded, and a presence were waiting,
        watching, patiently devoid of impulse or haste—
People hear the common tongue of love, the universal language
        of mortal things, soft, like a baby's voice,
        passing from person to person, pulsing from
        trees and grass and animals, connecting
        existence with existence.

Through the universal silent sound of mortal joy, individual life
                becomes bonded, tolerable, and touched.
Aware of this,
You can never speak up too often with the love of all things.

In the heart of every hunter, silence breaker, mass murderer, taker
                of life big or small
Is static.
Due to this static, they cannot hear the voices of all things babbling,
                crying, speaking from the heart;
Due to this static, some people cannot hear the way that tall grass stems
                sing lullabies to their neighboring grass; or
                the ways that birds, anxious, fretful, diligent,
                chase after their new-flown fledglings with
                morsels of food, or with admonitions of danger.
Those who are bedeviled by the static give it names that please them.
They befriend and flatter the static; calling it god, praising it as
                a folkway or as an heirloom.
They say the power of the static in their minds exempts them from the laws of love.
The deer hunter feels enthroned above the animals—he has forgotten,
                lost touch with, cannot feel the way the
                doe turns to nuzzle along in haste the fawn,
                heart-beating, eager to spur it on towards
                safety.
The terrorist, ethnic cleanser, nationalist, religionist, invoke the names
                and ideas of old books and imposing buildings.
They are deaf to the inaudible, dumb to the unspoken common tongue.
Listening to static and lost to love they kill the Jews of Europe, the Tutsis
                of East Africa, the intelligentsia of Cambodia, the

elephants of the Congo, the orangutans of Borneo, the
Atlantic, Pacific and Arctic whales.
Killing is indiscriminate and everywhere, the excuse changes, the reason
changes, the alleged necessity changes.
Therefore, you can never speak up too often for the love of all things.

Here is a pond on a summer afternoon, its water iridescent green
and blue beneath the long bright solar rays,
And here is a young man and young woman dipping into the water,
merging their bodies with the body of the pond.
From long ago they ran from hunters; as deer they ran from men with
painted faces and burning torches in the
Pleistocene night;
As rabbits they ran from dripping dogs;
For generations, their ancestors were Jewish runners, homeless here and
there across the landmass of Europe, chased by
people with a dozen different pedigrees.
As Africans they came in chains.
As trees, they were cut down at their feet, and fell on their faces.

Today, the pond skin shimmers in ecstacy of love as the breeze draws
its fingers across the water's surface.
The young man and the young woman dip into the pond's original and
fathomless watery womb.
And their child, who years later comes to the pond, dives in
all sweat and muscle, bull-necked from
mowing in the field,
His jeans and hair are jumbled with hay stems of daisies and wild pinks.

For each and every presence, place, person, animal, plant, on this earth,
there is someone who wants to kill or destroy them,
And there is also a great and universal love inside them, a love and
joy entwined, like a young man after a day's
work diving into a summer pond,
Like water, green, blue, clear, murky, impenetrably old primal element
of life, catching him, bathing him, whispering to
him unbeknownst to him himself, the secret and
universal words:

You can never speak up too often for the love of all things.

India

India, the Magnet Land

January 11, 2000

Incomprehensibly aloft and light, I, a land mammal
                with beard,
Ride alive in the cavern of this 747, thirty-thousand feet above
                the dark and swallowing Atlantic
Towards India, the magnet land.

Is my life a product of curiosity and cultural exchange,
                of a time when Westerners went East?
Or, is my life flowing from a past cause, that destined me to carry back,
                flight by flight,
The ancient light of India to the hemispheric West?

Year after year, stage after stage of life, I am called to ride
                the nauseating and magical jumbo jets.
Like a merchant after goods, like a bucket to be filled . . .
A purpose holds me hard, and I soar
Incomprehensibly aloft and light
Towards India, the magnet land.

Crossing time zones in rapid sequence I sleep
                at supper, wake at nightfall,
                doze at dawn.

Sky travel evaporates the arbitrary lines which people draw
     to imprison time and space.
The placeless dark outside the airplane window steals
     my land, my name, my century.

The phosphorescing cabin streaks across the unzoned sky.
Our only thread to human time is signals
Bleeped from distant air controls below.
The plane inside is glowing like a giant firefly
Directed by invisible planetary pheromones.
And I, like a soft and sleepy inner organ,
Am elevated to the peer of Zeus or Indra, as I
Defy gravity in quest of my blessed goal:
Incomprehensibly aloft and light
Towards India, the magnet land.

The landmass of Eurasia slowly glides below.
The Alps stab upward as if to halt the sky.
Is that snow in Macedonia, desert in Turkey?
These names and places cannot restrain the flow of tides.
Era after era, life after life, something is drawn on,
Incomprehensibly aloft and light
Towards India, the magnet land.

It's not a jet I ride, but mind,
Mind focused on its goal.
Thought drawing towards its object, across time and space,
Pulled by an imprint irresistible within my brain,
That matches outer form.

Pulled and pulling, a thread is reeled from either end
And I close in on India, the magnet land.

It is not the turbaned, bickering taxi drivers of Mumbai streets,
The naked toddlers chasing hoops in three-lane traffic,
The air, confined in a grill-work of corrosive pollutants —
This India of dust is not my orbit's hub.

The India that pulls me on, got charged
When the Big Bang lit the universe and threw
All molecules into their speed.

This magnet India formed its force
When the lights of heaven first curled their arc
Above the horizon, and all things were born.
Then truth became powerful, a field like gravity itself,
To pull and shape the stuff of things aeon after aeon,
Until out of matter's core a man congealed
On the little ball of earth.

There he sat.
Amidst the burning incandescence of the world
He spoke for the arising and vanishing
Inside of every thing.
In him, the universe saw its own confines.
He gave a voice, a phrase, a comprehensible refrain
To the processes that drive all things.
He spoke the words the universe implies.

When he died, a magnet formed where all things tend
When they dissolve without clinging or complaint.
He spoke the words the universe implies.
The earth he walked on magnetized.
To hear his words,
To watch my lives arise and not abide
I fly
Incomprehensibly aloft and light,
Towards India, the magnet land.

Dhamma Giri

I walk softly on your holy ground, Dhamma Giri, Mother Vipassana
               Center of the world,
Mindfully treading your paths and alleys, aware of the treasured esteem
               in which you are held
By meditators from every continent.
But you are not always so delicate and pristine.
Continuously in the process of being built . . . concrete mixers whirr
               along your edges,
New residences hover half-framed upon the roof-tops of old ones,
Small, muscular men in Gandhi-caps scrape mortar onto bricks,
               chip and fit flagstones,
               wail away at iron reinforcing rods
               with mauls ringing metallic
               on the heads of shivering chisels;
And redshawled, miniature women carry cracked stones in baskets
               on their heads
To build your dining halls and huts.

Dhamma Giri, I have stained my feet and cuffs with your russet dust,
Clumsily chased my hat across your wind-buffeted plateaus,
Coughed and sneezed up your smoke and soil-rich air,
And walked in silence for a month along your tree-lined lanes,
Seeking to return to love and equanimity.

In front of your dining hall, my sandal, in undignified rebuff,
          refuses to slide gracefully off my bent left big-toe;
And as I stir, pinioned, around me glide the forms of old men from Maharashtra,
          young Buddhist monks from Burma,
          towering Germans in their cavalier Birkenstocks;
Until at last my toe slips free and I step forward to feel
The barefoot plantar touch of India:
Foot-worn paving stones, smoothed by anonymous multitudes of feet,
Uneven rock, still somewhere inside itself heaving with the tumult
          of the earth that birthed it aeons ago,
But now cool and calmed by naked human tread,
And bearing on its stony surface the fine, ubiquitous, signature grit,
          that tells my toes,
You have arrived; you are back home again.

Now I throw in my lot, Dhamma Giri, with the barefoot pilgrims
          from around the world
Who have come to meditate Vipassana amidst the dust and rock
          of your holy elemental ground!

Dhamma Giri, mother of rock, dust, sun, and dark, where would you be
          without your pagoda,
That strange and dominating form?
It sprang up from the mind of your teacher, your Guru,
          whose concentration and faith envisioned you.
He dreamed the dream of your upward thrusts and curves appearing
          into this physical world;
And tenaciously over relentless years, the pagoda emerged in slow magic,
          like a mother giving birth

from the sphere of mind
to your earthly plane of peace.
Dhamma Giri, you and your pagoda are the materialization
in brick, concrete, and marble
of a seer's inner sight.

The pagoda towers over you, its gilded golden dome arresting every eye,
Its squat, circular base tapering upward in conical ascent to its turret
of shining light and tinkling wind-bells,
That attract celestial moods to its regal heights.
And around the pagoda base, like ripples from a stone, in concentric rings,
hundreds of tiny cells spread out,
Encircling each inner row, in casual architectural aplomb,
Each tiny cell-roof tipped with floral lotus peak.
This is no building. It's a lab, a greenhouse of the heart.

The pagoda is the hub of the eternal experiment
of life shedding its separateness
And opening unreservedly to love and equanimity.
In many a world cycle, in many a cosmic birth and death,
this effort has gone on:
Those who know their transiency, and purify their personality,
until self-clinging's gone.
Here, Dhamma Giri, we repeat the truth this time around:
all things decay.
The Unborn has no form.

Each pagoda cell provides full privacy,
Yet all face center where the teacher sits.

Each meditator in darkness and closed eyes faces every other cell,
        yet none can see.
Alone, together, each meditator is tuned by the pagoda's orbic vibe.

When I return to sit in your dark cells, the agitated motion of my mind stills.
I close the door and cross my legs.
Now I wrap the shawl of truth around me,
And seek to realize, moment by moment, in the scintillation of my body's life,
Reality of change upon change, the chemistry of life,
The atomic, kinetic base of incessant transformation
In the particles of myself.

Dhamma Giri, I sit in your timeless, lightless, morning and afternoon
        pagoda meditation cells,
To find impermanence manifesting in every molecule of myself,
And so to spring free of believing in that self,
Which I exchange
For love and equanimity.

Slowly, slowly, when I am not sitting, I traverse your hilltop land, Dhamma Giri,
        and feel your loving strength
          beneath my every step.
When my mind runs wild like a caged rodent seeking *out*,
        your cool and tree-lined path that lies within
        Arañña-gato vā, having gone to the forest,
Cups and buffers my hot distress like a mother's soothing hand.
When I walk with concentrated intent and downcast eyes in dusk
        toward your lecture hall,

The pagoda's wind-chimes silver-plate my mind with moonlight
        and stellar psalms.
When I meditate upstairs, in your highest cells, nearest the Teacher's own,
        great waves of love and equanimity
Surge towards me from the center of invisible worlds.

No, you are not all detachment and solemnity, Dhamma Giri; you catch
        the ruckus of the world.
From the town side of your hilly walls, upward floats the roar of tractors,
        claxons of taxis, hoots and hisses of trains,
        the blare of movie music and religious congregational excitation,
        magnified through megaphones.
On your village edge, the dusk brings rise and fall, like surf,
        of children always in groups and games;
        or songs of a solitary radio;
        and cows, lowing in the stubble of rice paddy.
At night you often pulse with the paleo-rhythmic drive of distant
        and placeless drums and chanting.

And everywhere you have crows: crows cawing, crows squawking
        in lugubrious, untranslatable dialogue back and forth
        between two trees in the glaring afternoon sun;
Crows gathering in cacophonous mobs that blacken the treetops at dusk,
Crows on the roofs, crows rustling leaves, crows with their bills
        wacking over metal drinking cups
        that fall and clatter repetitively
        during the supposedly silent
        evening discourse hour,
Crows waddling down walkways like men,

Crows punctuating endless hot afternoons with their metronomic calls:
        walk walk; walk walk;
Crows bringing black irreverent life and motion into your calm pool
Of stillness, austerity, and self-effacing rectitude.

But, Dhamma Giri, above you always stands, from noon to starry night,
        the great black mesa.
Towering thousands of feet above you, parched, impersonal as a tombstone,
        a mountain, ageless
        beyond any human hope.
That is why, a thousand years ago, Buddhist monks carved out caves
        in solid rock cliffs,
Among the range of ravaged, eerie mountains that lie behind the mesa,
        and that remain
        so wild and untamed.
This is the land that calls the human heart to meditate upon eternal and immediate
        change upon change.
From here, those long-gone monks could radiate the world with the
        compassionate blessings
        of their deep remove,
That pulses from them still, like the last measurable wavelength of isotopic decay.
As real time blots out short human spans,
Above each meditator on your grounds
That mountain mesa's black bulk measures out true magnitude.

Why do I keep returning to you, Dhamma Giri, where I waste unmonkish time
        ambling down mental valleys
        of deeply encrusted daydreams;

Where I strive the whole month through to hold the body's relentless change in view,
         only to feel the time
Evaporate into lost moments beyond the mesh of memory?
I hear you repeat over and over to me, Dhamma Giri, just one message,
         which is:
We can always return to love and equanimity.

Every time I arrive upon your gated grounds,
And every time I depart,
I feel beneath me ineluctably the trickery of fate.
I treat you as a one-time thing.
I never know if health, disease, war or politics
May seal you off from me.
But I carry your message in my back and bones.
Whatever happens outside (I hear you say to me)
Inside our own bodies we can always return
To love and equanimity.

So grand, so vigorously and caringly built, you too, Dhamma Giri,
         will crumble and pass on some day.
A thousand years from now, people may tell legends of the students
         who thronged your atmosphere of quietude
Coming from every country on the globe:
         The United Nations of Meditation.

Where will I be then, a thousand years from now, in what form,
         with what worry still on my mind,

What sort of body will I be that

Somewhere in the fine, atomic, vibratory structure I will hold and hear

> your one gift to me:

The practice, the faith, to restore awareness

Through direct experience of insubstantiality:

We can always return to love and equanimity.

> Oh, dear old Dhamma Giri,
> We will praise you wordlessly
> By the way we walk through life.

> Let our days make us worthy of your stones and dust.

Meditation

Islands in the Storm

Dhamma Suttama, little meditation center on the hill
        among the maples
In Quebec, where everything has two names —
        there are deer and chevreuil in the woods,
        students and etudiants in the meditation hall —
Where as soon as I speak, someone echoes me in Frankish harmonies.
Here you can inhale the sweet exhalation of grass and trees;
        the air is scented breath that has been
        minted inside the bodies
        of respiring summer foliage.
This is the land where the Appalachians peter out
From their long rumpled folds in the U.S.A.
Large lumps of low mountains built up
        among the flat plateaus.
Even the continents were once storm waters, wild
        synclines and anticlines aeons ago,
        squirming and buckling on the globe.
Now this worn down Northland has just the right incline
        to hold a meditation center
        on its flanks;
Dhamma Suttama, high and afloat amidst the surf of North America,
        like an island in the storm.
America and Canada collide here sleepily.

Ten days of silent sitting hard and still, forty people
        in the small, woodbeamed hall,
Each facing a gale of inner woe and pain with the strength
        of equanimity,
Built upon the realization of impermanence of every sensation
        of the body/mind,
Every etudiant here is striving to be an island in the storm.
As we meditate day after day . . . morning, noon, and evening
        pass us by like sailboats
        upon an inland sea.
We ride the waves alone together, our multilingual pirate band
        holding tight to our seats,
        as we row between the crests
        of birth and death,
Stealing golden coins of peace from moments in the squalls of time.
Each of us has buried treasure on this island in the storm.
Upon the round ocean of the world, in India, Nepal,
        Mongolia, Taiwan, New Zealand, Australia,
        Germany, France, Japan
(their clocks reversed, their buildings shaped to different architectural design),
Other meditation centers house other bands of voyageurs,
        who sail upon the seas of land.
An archipelago of meditation centers spans the planet now,
Among the heavy continents where all humanity is born.
We are all alone together, living islands in the storm.

One Last River's Wild Ride

When you are paddling a canoe through rapids, you need to go faster than the water in order to retain autonomous mobility, free of the current.

It's as if we are always paddling down a river, you and I,
        who are always in the same boat,
Canyon walls towering above us on either side, and no way off the water,
        so forced right down the chute,
White water below us—certain death—
And instead of just collapsing into inevitable, undignified defeat,
We accelerate the boat's descent!

Dig the paddles deep into the black back of water!
Let's outrace the current down towards the dark rocks and wild foam,
Ahead of the game, source of our own speed,
Let's lean out beyond the gunnels, the better to brace and bend
        the responsive ash paddle blades,
Swirling our canoe with living heat of muscle's inner fire,
Past rock after menacing rock's destructive rim,
We're wheeling, urging on,
Our deltoids flaring out like flanks of wild horses
As we sweep down the white water's heaving, surging mass.

For the person truly alive, death must be a victory we approach
        at our own speed,

Inevitable, looming ahead.
Let's not be taken down, but shoot across in full possession
          of the final moment's facts.
Either then, or long before then,
Even right now, we may awaken
Into true river boaters,
Always paddling towards the last moment
With a spirit that moves faster than the water and so retains command
          over motility and the mind's lithe moves,
As we yell over to our companion paddler above the river's roar,
"This river trip's my dream come true."

In my body, I am landlocked, decaying from within and greying from without,
Knees grinding against time-worn cartilages,
Head of the humerus no longer able to rotate within the scapula's rounded,
          roughened bed,
Spinal column rotting like damp basement sills—
A patriarch I've never seen before stares back at me from among his silver
          beard and mane
As I comb my hair in the mirror every morning.
But in spirit I feel new born.
Now I want to take my life
As one last river's wild ride.
You and me, old travelers, old adventurers,
Howling on North Woods lakes along with loons, haloed by pastel sunsets,
Alert and upright in the bucking boat,
Facing every submerged boulder, every eddy
With total contact of our body, mind, and paddles,
Far, far beyond mere faith—
Living to our last immersed
In one last river's wild ride.

The paddler heads down the river towards where it dips below the line of sight—
Watches the liquid world of his own body scintillate around him in roiling
                ricochets and runs,
Stripped of everything but realization now
All-grasping wrung out of him,
His mind open like the original dawn,
The great determination of the paddler pays off at last,
Powers concentration and unblinking recognition of the truth.
Now is the time for fruition within the storm,
Wisdom while rushing down the rapids
Totally calm, alert acceptance of reality:
This is the way the riverman descends
On his one last river's wild ride.

Inside the mind is a river of thought and turbulent water—
Despairs and pity and pleas ready to crack the distracted or hesitant boat.
But you and I, let's be hell-bent to become
Old river boaters, keen, fast and steady eyed,
Leaning forward, paddle blades churning, racing down white water
On one last river's wild ride.

There is Only One Exalted Emotion

For Mike and Shari, Guilford, July 17, 1999

I

There is only one exalted emotion
Just as there is only one clear light.

There is an exalted, presiding, universal emotion, that isn't ours,
    which pervades the world around us,
     into the radiance of which we can enter.
We step past a diaphanous curtain into a presence we have
    long dreamed of encountering.

There is only one energy so pure,
But like light passing through celestial vapor to form a
    rainbow,
This emotion can be separated into colors
We call love, joy, peace and compassion.
Whichever one of these four we feel,
We are in the presence of the other three also,
And are bathed in the nameless white light.

II

Deep peace is possible only to a heart inhabited by love, joy, and care.
How could peace hover in a house seething with hate;

        half-full of despair,

        or angrily armored?

Love only enters the heart on soft carpets of peace.
How could love enter and fill life's chambers

        whose floors were cluttered

        with the turbulent and the fretful?

Love and peace steam the winter windows with joy —

        like the belly laugh of the toddler

        with his mother in a room full of toys.

Then compassion flings open the front gate:
We wander the neighborhood, knocking on doors, garrulous,
Eager to share our gift, which is a household
Lit by the one clear light.

III

There is only one exalted emotion
Just as there is only one hub of a wheel.
All sacred life rotates around this center.
The universe is a boy who opens his hand and casts down his wrist

        in one fluid sweeping motion

And the yo-yo spins.
To find the one exalted emotion let go
Let it drop.
When we stop clinging, one exalted emotion whirls inside us.

IV

Meditation is an arched doorway into the temple of exaltation.

When we enter its domed recesses

Our shoulders loosen,

We forget our craving for a future,

And ceasing to grasp,

We breathe in full awareness, insubstantial, incandescent:

Glowing wave-fields of vivacity without form.

Then we forget to remember our name.

Everything is enough.

V

We can never contain the one exalted emotion—instead

      we abide under its great suzerainty.

Its four sons steal into the party of guests in our household

      speaking wise, courteous, soothing words to

      our friends.

Its four daughters instruct our offspring of thoughts, words, and deeds.

VI

There is only one exalted emotion that extends love without exception to

      all suffering beings,

That sends joy surging through and past us like a spring flood,

That stirs compassion never placated nor finished,

That brings peace from infinitely far in the past traveling infinitely far into

      the future while hovering inside us

      motionlessly.

The joys and sorrows of this life are decorations in the corridors of our dreams

But there is only one exalted emotion when we are awake.

VII

There is only one exalted emotion that is universal, not ours,
        which exists independently of us, into which
        we can enter, a pure energy containing love,
        joy, peace, and compassion in a rainbow.
I keep trying to grab onto it but it eludes me, passing between my
        fingers like life itself, with ineluctable transience.
But when my misguided grasping exhausts itself, I suddenly feel
        in my quiet heart and mind a door opening,
As if a small boy were peeking through a crack in the door
Into the room where his grandfather was meditating.

At that moment it seems, an all-powerful wind of love
        sweeps through the entire universe of my mind.
In every galaxy on every mental plane, I see all people, gods and living things
        reach out their arms with joy;
And peace rises up in every body in the world like a great, magnetic, uniform
        inhalation,
Suffusing the soft and beating heart of every child who has ever existed,
Suffusing the heart of every child who ever will exist.

Liberation is everywhere.
Glowing wave-fields of vivacity without form.
Everything is enough.

The Poet
is a Force of Nature

The Poet is a Force of Nature

For Makarand Dave

The poet is a force of nature, like the ocean and the clouds.

In the arteries and veins of the poet flows the universal common language,
         of which the sounds, words, and grammar
        that we call languages
        are only dialects.
English, Gujarati, Spanish, or Swedish are only the names of tributaries.
The river of the universal common language floats all poetry down
        from the mountains
        that tower in the heart of all things.

The vowels of poetry are created by young mothers fussing over and nuzzling
         their newborns;
And by the doves of Rajasthan, cooing hypnotically from the porticos
        of stone archways, on hot, timeless, desert afternoons.

The consonants of poetry derive from the surf, torch-singing to sunsets on all the
         beaches around the globe;
And from crickets, chiming their crystalline voices through chocolate, velvet,
        summer nights.

Streams flowing under bridges and over rocks speak every language in the world
and dictate the content of all poems.

Poets receive this language involuntarily.
They participate in a phenomenon they cannot control.
Beautiful phrases appear in their minds the way that songbirds suddenly appear
on the limbs of overhanging trees.

When all the citizens of nature are eating, flying, running, growing, reproducing,
chasing, scurrying, fighting,
How can the poet dare to spend the entire afternoon seated cross-legged
on the bed, propped up by pillows,
scribbling in a small notebook?

The poet has accepted this as his calling: to receive the jolt
of sacred irruptions
from the reality that lies beyond.

Open and receptive to the whole world, the poet is lofted upward like a raptor
on outspread wings,
And he circles the farms, field, and civilizations from above, looking for
telltale movements.

When he speaks from within his sphere of influence, he points towards
massive and inevitable realities,
like soil, rain, and pregnant women,
from which all that is fertile and subsequent derives.

His message is indiscriminate joy in the perception of reality without flinching.

Amidst the primal terrors that grip and rend humankind—war, violence,
                    delusion, disease, and death—
The poet, like a redemptive ray of sunlight, pierces each and every person,
                    more or less,
Transmitting from generation to generation, fundamental truths and feelings
                    that instill a degree of harmony and faith.

His topic is compassion: life itself like a May-born robin fallen onto the grass.
His context is cosmic, every person suspended in a cat's cradle hung over corners
                    of the galaxies.
His chorus is selfless detachment amidst eternal change.

The poet is a force of nature that never dies.
After the breath ceases, poets dive down beneath the visible wavelengths
Into the realm of eternal and inaudible voices that are the source
                    of sacred irruptions
                    from the reality that lies beyond.

Perception

I

Walking trails on Mt. Toby I perceive
Every square yard of ground perfected.

Rocks. Squirrel-nibbled white pine cones.
Paisley shaped necks and pods of mud,
And the patterned placement of wildflowers.

Today every detail appears to be
The culmination of eternal artistry:
Messages, symbols, manifestations of the law.

The inevitable, exact, exquisite, precision
Of cosmic evolution
Manifesting in littoral profusion.

These woods and the world
Seem a puzzle of inexplicably interwoven
Articulation and conclusion.
A mixture of the clock and the jewel.

Every anonymous wild white anemone
Is a well-tooled screw
In the functioning machinery
Of the galactic evolution of planet earth.
Displace a wildflower and you would topple the gods.

II

My thoughts also seem
Exact, beautiful, luminous
With all meanings compiled and summated.

But I remember other minds I carry other days,
Minds like streets of Newark,
Stark and ugly concrete, crashed beer bottles,
Trash barrels overflowing.
Then again I sometimes saw the slums
Of Newark, Chicago, Pittsburgh
Strewn with broken glass
Reflect a Byzantine mosaic designed
By a higher hand: and ghetto streets
Had secret beauties and patina pavement churches.

III

Today as I wander the June woods,
Trailside patches of wild geraniums
Remind me of the way that Neal—
Long dead of AIDS—once helped Auntie—
Now long dead of stroke—over the mud
And poison ivy among the lavender geraniums

On the day that you and I
Got married in the pinewoods.

We live, we die, we never know
If order lurks inside events.
All perception, all conclusion
Contains the tints of self-deceit and flattery.

There are echoes inside the patterns of my thoughts:
Old footfalls, voices across a lake,
The laconic spoken rhythms of the American patois.

All we have is love and intermittent equanimity
In a world of patterns and impermanence.
Anemones, geraniums, and fading human faces
In the mirrors of my mind.

A Remote and Exquisite Peace

Cloaked in joy, I wander among the shadows and the phosphorescence,
Transmuting life into language.

The passage of time, the passing of life, is the one true reality.
Any goal that we have ever attained,
Any shame festering at our pit,
Finally passes into oblivion.
Memory fades, the river of time surges on, our bodies decay,
                exalted and treasured moments of mindful
                alertness nevertheless become long-forgotten
                non-memories of graveless past lives.
In spite of this, defiantly,
Forces of knowing enter into us, hollow us, pry open our consciousness
To receive ultimate truth.
Reality penetrates our ignorance on underground rivers of time, loss, change.

Then to what meaningful purpose can the tool of my mind be turned?
What is this continuous recognition, the formation of verbs and nouns,
                transcription of reality into ionized sounds?
The poetry of rocks and rivers is my mind's natural activity.
A remote and exquisite peace
Turns all moments over and over like rounded river stones,
                smoothed and shining.

In the mind's clearest moments, everything that has transpired
                seems perfect.
All words ripple downstream as liberating poetry.
Every pebble and stone sparkles with precious minerals.
Resting by uncountable billions in the beds of all rivers
                are rolled, rounded stones and poems.

In the deepest meditation, edges disappear,
All memories become rounded by charitable acceptance,
All turmoil subsides to undulating rivers washing over beds
                of rounded stones.
Rushing towards open seas are poems of remote and exquisite peace.

Resolutions for Citizens
of the New Age of Earth

Resolutions for Citizens of the New Age of Earth

Let us meditate every morning and evening as reliably as the sun
            observes dawn and dusk.
Let us cohabit in sanctity with all life, even as far as coexisting with
            the big spider who was dangling on a thread
            in front of my bathroom mirror this morning.
Let all plants and animals be known as our kin.
Let us procreate and populate like gardeners, aware that the earth is a space
            which can be filled, and that children thrive
            on deep, sustained, skillful attention and affection.
Let our religion be reduced to this: love creates love; hate creates hate;
            peace creates peace.

Let us hone our bodies for health, refraining from meat, drinking tea,
            hiking, running, doing yoga, while we
            keep in mind that the greatest joys in life
            come winging over to us during moments
            of uncontrolled, receptive pause. Let's sit.
Let all occasions be opportunities.
Let us search for the right word, the honest sentence, the powerful but
            considerate phrasing.
Let us make every moment and every interaction a source point of listening
            and concern, but let our perspective expand
            from immediacies to stretch beyond constellations and
            light-years. There are more than one hundred

billion galaxies with more than one hundred
billion stars, and we don't even live long
enough to be able to ever once count to one billion.
Perspective is a microscope and a telescope.
Remembering that right now is the culmination of previous eternity
from beginningless time, and that right now is the
origin of all future time, let's keep trying to fill our
kitchens with the smell of fresh baked bread.

Let us parry the assault upon us of tribalism, self-righteousness and conviction,
with our playful irreverence and enviable delight.
Let us speak up in a conversational tone of voice about the universality of
life and the universality of death, the two
common attributes shared by all living things.
Among the surging tides of demands and provocations, let us gather among
our friends under the shawl of silence and peace.

Let us approach the great inanimant beings of this planet,
the mountains and rivers, as teachers.
Let them strike us with the awe of their age,
the majesty of their dimensions, the sacredness
of the opportunity to be alive on the earth.
Let us cherish them as personal friends.
Let us listen to the deep pulsing prayers they chant unceasingly.

Let us make pilgrimages in the company of four-year-old children to waterfalls.
Let us wander around the woods in May, to become saturated by the
parental joy of singing birds. Let us enter
their forests like cathedrals.

May we outgrow our primitive desires, and become increasingly
        transparent vehicles for love, joy, peace, and
        compassion.
May we walk the path towards *nibbāna,* the absence of hate, passion and
        fear; and may this faith in the potential for
        human goodness (from which we ourselves
        deviate so often) remain our one naive,
        unshakable, overbelief.
May we have faith in the enduring fecundity of the seeds that have
        sprouted from our own small successes.

Let us surrender our life with calm, dignity, and gratitude for what
        we've had, not dismay about what is passing.
Until then
let reverence be our guide to becoming citizens for the new age of earth.

Even if we don't let all of these things happen, let them happen anyway.

Jātaka Tale

The Buddha taught fables, Jātaka tales, to reinforce simple morality.

In America, we are subservient to hunting, its legendary augmentation of
          prowess, the myth of Daniel Boone,
As if today, in our computer-run, global society of six billion souls, a man
          could prove his worth, by crushing something furry.
This exercise is left to those who have no other source of self-esteem than to
          elevate themselves
          on the broken bodies of vanishing species;
And the extermination of animals is justified as sportsmanship.

In my idea of sportsmanship, there'd have to be true sport,
          like soccer teams with equal odds.
I'd want to arm all the animals and airfauna equal and opposite.
The aggregate mammals and game birds of North America would have a
          nuclear arsenal adequate
To exterminate the earth one thousand times over, just as we Americans do.
I'd feel safer in the hands of nuclear bears, big mighty beasts, already used
          to the limited and judicious exercise of power;
Or moose, who thoughtfully threaten, display, and pose to warn, before they attack.
Polar bears in their white majesty would command aircraft carriers with
          nuclear tipped missiles,
But would launch them sparingly, spearing and roasting a man or two, only for
          food;

Their ursine, polar parliament would deem the slaughter of us *OK*, as long

        as they'd make use of all our hides, no waste, and a season's

        take limited to three in a bag.

Wait! I've become alarmed at my own suggestions, imagining nuclear warheads

        in the hands

Of some red squirrels I've encountered in Maine, their teeth chattering in rage,

Their bushy tails flicking back and forth in hysterical fury aimed at me as

        I walk beneath their red pine tree limb.

Imagine a cruise missile in the hands of a skunk.

How would we all feel looking up to see a flight of mallards sweeping over

        the thawing marshes of March—what might they be

        hiding in their posterior down?

Overall, I still like my plan—a mighty Vee of geese would command

        the respect they deserve from uppity man.

If we armed the beasts to the teeth as we are, most humans would resume

        their age-old love of and reverence for

The common life of animality.

In any case, the last human hunters would be gone, selectively harvested one by one

        by the smart bombs computer-guided to their targets

From command posts among the relict herds of bison on the American Great Plains;

And human males would go on vision quests to prove their prowess by negotiating

        peaceful settlements with the great cats—

        cougar, lion, tiger, and jaguar.

Boys would follow their fathers through the autumn woods with numbers on their

        orange hats, to crunch the colored leaves,

Seeking to capture the tang of frost and apples on the barbed tips of ancient

        Anglo-Saxon words—

All of humankind would at last aspire to meditation and poetry.
Real men would hang the first lines of sonnets over their mantlepiece as trophies.

And around our domes of love and peace, where cross-legged meditators
                radiate their consanguineous joy,
Armed wolves would stalk to protect us from ourselves,
And grizzly bears would police the nightmares that once
                propelled humanity to violence.
Humanism would have died with Fascism and Communism,
Animalism and Plantism would be our common ground.
Fur would be no liability, affection no shame,
And underground testing would be affirmed
As the realm and prerogative of beetles and worms.

Costa Rica

Scarlet Macaws

Sometimes nature seems to break all her rules.

A flight of scarlet macaws above the tops of the coconut palms
                that line the Pacific beach at Marenco, Costa Rica,
A rippling parade of birds, rivaling the rainbow, long tails streaming
                behind them,
Birds surfing on a tide of color that is normally invisible, but whose
                wave crests are now revealed to waft giant
                avians along in multicolored, roller coaster glee,
Raucous, screeching, demanding that the entire assemblage of man and nature
                turn to receive the shock and delight of their
                gaudy red, blue, and yellow plumage,
Showing off in defiance of all laws of integration, blending in,
                camouflage,
Not even regal or princely, but an outlandishly breathtaking rupture
                of natural relationships—
I believe these long-tailed fliers have come to reveal to me an extreme
                and unimaginable potential
                never before realized in the world,
Scarlet macaws, shattering the subdued and seasoned harmonics of
                steely ocean, tan sand, white clouds,

With their spectrum-spanning pigments, attention-riveting squawks,
        and aerial antics,
They turn the whole world giddy at the elastic potential
        within creation.

How must the scarlet macaws appear to the little riverside wren
        we saw in the seaside bushes this morning,
        or to all the tribes of ground-dwelling ant-birds,
        wood creepers, and thrushes,
Small brown things, barely able to raise a stripe, sneaking along
        the forest floor in a life of timidity,
        obscurity and prudence,
Looking up to see their decorum mocked, their caution discarded,
        their careful cultivation of nonentityness
        jettisoned
By these ribald, exhibitionistic macaws, scattered in crayola abandon?

And what would I see, what would it mean to me, if one person,
        or a small group of people, were to envision
        human life carried as far towards ultimate freedom,
        as macaws have done with feather, voice, and flight?
It wouldn't be—for a human—just some harlequin apparel or strident voices;
And such sensuous, gravity-defying flight as macaws have would be impossible
        for a person, and in any case a merely
        physical attainment.

What if a human being were to attain some equally, and previously
        unimaginable flight of the spirit?
What if a person could analogously tease out to its maximum our human potential?

What then would I see, what magic would be revealed on sky, beach, or earth?

Was Einstein a macaw? Was there some manifestation of macaw-ness

in the art of Rembrandt when he induced living light

to emerge from the eyes of painted portraits?

Van Gogh may have carried in his retina that same expanded jubilation

in chromatics, as the splendid fliers I saw

this morning lofting above the beach at dawn.

The macaws, after all, are not really rule breakers, but revelations,

physical representations of how far the laws of nature

can be stretched.

What other attributes of heart and mind can yet be drawn newborn

from nature's untapped well?

When human beings extend equally far nature's catalytic sacred secrets,

but in a human mode,

On that day will be revealed a vast expansion of the spectra of love and reason.

Not one alone, imbalanced, heart or mind, but most magnificent human wings,

symmetrical,

Love and reason, beating towards one goal,

Undulating in exquisite attainment across the horizons of history.

There have already been, and will be again, such people,

Who reach out wide to the ultimate edge,

Who fly above fear and joy, birth and death,

To soar beyond suffering, its cause, its end, on the air waves transcending it;

People who have seen and can describe insights of the greatest height,

total freedom of flight, ocean crossing,

unbrooked, released!

This measured, balanced, duo, the good and the real, carry people as far
        as humans ever grow or need to,
Aloft in winged wisdom on the greatest human enterprise: to be free,
        and to reach out a helping hand.

Macaws mate for life. They fly as bird and wife,
Pairs within the soaring flocks,
Then depart, leaving me alone to watch the emptied beach, the impersonal waves,
        the distant and unreachable heights of the Cordillera Talamanca,
        mountains volcanic born and risen
        in some unthinkably ancient expansive era
        when the Western Hemisphere itself was reaching for the sky.
Now the Talamancas rumble down the spine of the American north-south
        supercontinent, inland from me.
I am a lonely man, always wandering, wondering how we, my species-tribe,
        can grow wise and sweet,
And so become at last obedient
To the vast mystery of peace
That occasionally emerges amidst the infinity of things.

Somehow, something, somewhere has lifted a curtain inside my mind.
In the accumulating morning light I see streamers,
Red, blue, and yellow semaphores of hope
For a great flight of love and reason to rise from the beach and undulate
        towards final liberation
Inside all of our shared and solitary lives.

A Small Brown Bird

Jardin Wilson, San Vito, Costa Rica

for Bosque
". . . some of the small brown birds are the most beautiful
when you really observe them carefully . . ."

A young woman stood transfixed at the edge of a mighty river that
                 rushed past her.
Across the river from her, mountain ranges ran from North to South,
                 rugged, towering, cloud-festooned,
                 as far as the eye could see in either direction.
And there was only one thought on the young woman's mind: awareness.
She pondered the origin, evolution, purpose, goal, import, method, plan,
                 process, of every plant, animal,
                 river, mountain, ocean and continent on
                 her planet.
Behind the young woman, in rows, in mobs, in aggregate mass,
                 humanity was pushing, grabbing, yelling,
                 demanding, shoving to get past her, to
                 cross the river and the mountains;
But the young woman focused her awareness upon a small brown
                 bird creeping up a tree trunk, cocking its
                 head this way and that in search of insects,
And humanity remained halted behind her.

A young man stood at the edge of a rushing river which flowed past
        the feet of majestic mountain crests running
        North and South to the horizons;
And in the young man's heart was only one feeling: reverence
For all the lives, phenomena, manifestations of existence, whose origins defy
        knowledge, whose goals transcend conceptualization,
        and whose myriad forms wander across the surface
        of the planet, as insects, plants, animals, clouds, and people.
Behind the young man, humanity, six billion bodies, idling their cars,
        honking, yelling out from their rolled-down windows,
        arguing over religion, economics, politics and dreams,
        waiting, waited for him to get out of the way
        so they could move on across;
But the young man's heart was focused on a cloud fragment that had drifted
        away from the tumultuous thunderheads forming
        around the mountain ridge, and he watched
        the white banner trail down an
        alpine valley;
And humanity remained halted behind him.

The young woman thought to herself: I will not defer to authority,
        data, status, even genius;
But I will increase my direct, unmediated awareness of life;
        and I will be a teacher, encouraging
        others to do the same.
At that moment the earth shook and split open.
Out from the earth's core poured legions of birds, beasts, butterflies,
        flying, fleeing, fluttering freely through the wilderness
        slopes of the great mountain range.

The young man thought to himself: I will not believe any book,
       tradition, explanation or reduction.
I will open my whole being, mind and body, to receive in direct,
       unmediated experience the impact of the world
       in unmoderated communion and wonder;
       and I will be a teacher, encouraging
       others to do the same.
At that moment, the ripple of forest leaves chanted in harmonic chorales;
       the pattern of random roots and debris
       on the woodland floors cohered
       into calligraphically emblazoned, scriptural, poetry;
       and phrases of hallowed thoughts were traced across the sky
       by wisps of cloud and wind.

Now humanity moved forward slowly, asking, querying, observing,
       studying, knowing nothing and deferentially curious.
Life forms flowed like caribou herds across an isthmus, and wherever on
       any scale there was a gap, synapse, space, or void,
       living beings crossed, not just on earth, but on
       numberless planets, solar systems, galaxies, universes
       and multiverses.

Every existent being, large or small, simultaneously realized the unaccountable
       presence of existence to be opportune.
Joy scintillated like background radiation through the yawning caverns of
       cosmic distances.
Every living being everywhere understood that its individual life was a
       vehicle to transmit through time and space
       awareness and reverence.

Gods spontaneously dissolved. One young man and one young woman had
                 become sufficient to deify life everywhere.
Everyone understood why small brown birds exist.

One small brown bird climbed up a trunk of an old hardwood in
                 a deep tropical forest, turning its head this
                 way and that to search for insects.
A young woman observed its habits, its gestures, its motions.
A young man absorbed the mottled, subtle pattern of muted colors
                 in its feathers.
Seeing this, the entire universe inverted like a sock.
And out of its ageless mind all the wisdom and kindness
                 remembered from all locations,
                 and from all eras of time, blew in a delicate pinpoint breeze
                 onto one point of space.
Every moment there had ever been of awareness and reverence coalesced
                 into a small brown bird, with mottled
                 muted feathers, climbing up a treetrunk.

Gestation

Why does all this life exist—
Life penetrating everywhere, opulent and profuse, filling
               every niche, layer, and interstice,
Pulsing outward with its urgent code?

The rainforest is impenetrable to the eye.
A fortress of foliage, whose massive hardwood trunks
               like cathedral beams soar skyward.
My neck cranes back into dizziness as I try to realize the ascent
               of these shafts of wooden energy
               erupting upward from the forest floor
               in centuries-long ardor.
And the green: there are green curtains of monocots and dicots,
               great green blades and fans of leaves,
               long green philodendron tongues,
               and mossy green liverwort carpets
               lining treelimbs with fleece.
With its ferny architectural grill, and rhizomatous penetrance
Plant life seems everywhere, opulent and profuse.

Why does all this life exist?
White-faced capuchin monkeys stamping up and down
               in anti-human fury
               on canopy limbs;

Ant-thrushes teetering along the leaf-litter on the rainforest floor;
Leaf-cutter ants in winding columns like Napoleon's army
                waving green flags of leaf-fragments
                as they traverse old serpentine Roman roads
                leading from nowhere to nowhere
                in the forest's filagree;
Mosquitoes on my arm; no-see-ums on my legs;
                nameless kamikaze insect heroes
                committing the ultimate sacrifice
                in the corners of my eyes;
Animal life seems everywhere, opulent and profuse.

Each plant or animal emerged like a face peering from
                a seed or womb,
                of some chlorophyllic or winged ancestor.
Intergenerational landslide, life bore life in helpless excess and multiplicity,
Every living thing blessed and cursed,
Hungering, hunting, eating, thirsting,
Striving to maintain itself against the inevitable and always
                triumphant tug of individual demise,
All life in anxiety all day against death like a green skink
                racing across an open trail
                in flight from bird beak above.
From choiceless birth, and ceaseless self-maintaining quest,
                life edges into consciousness.

This consciousness with which I watch and seem to stand apart and think
Is it just life itself, more life, the ultimate adaptation?
Survival flung the disk of conscious mind

into a spinning and hovering
vigilance of knowing.
Is consciousness just the ultimate claw or beak:
Is consciousness no more than the caracara's high flight,
Extreme and irrepressible reach for life —
Is consciousness more a triumph than the iridescent ecstacy of light
on a hummingbird's breast?
What we call evolution
Is the ongoing glide of the desperate and the jubilant:
unexpected, endless, extreme.
Consciousness is no more unique than the governments of bees and ants,
or the thousand figure-eights
in the sabre-bill's wing beats.

But is this quirk of germs and genes that we call life a blind alley,
a phantom that raced too far
before crashing,
The length of its loops run out like a broken yo-yo?
All the rainy emerald growth of Costa Rica's lush banana hills
is cut, felled, burnt
to clear thorny cattle pasture
To raise rejected beef fit only for processed food.

All this life races towards a goal as chopped beef T.V. dinner.

Why does all this life exist, opulent, profuse, imperfect?
A platform, a pyramid, a broad scaffold of cells,
That slowly raises mist that we call mind
into the altitudes of highest thought.

A supreme, ethereal skim from the soup of algae and apes:

        elevated and transcendent.

The dense web of succulence and struggle suspends infinities of interactions,

From which all answers come eternally reconceived

Within the collision of all that's green and crawling.

The long, slow erection of life,

The trillion-fold parade of birth and death in manifold forms,

This may be the way enlightenment appears,

Like a slow bud opening into an orchid

Cellular life impregnated with self-detachment, care, and peace.

Maybe all of life is only the gestation period of love.

Maybe one day the rainy season clouds hovering above

        the hills around Coto Brus

        will coalesce

Into the perfect all-knowing boy.

Today on the muddy Rio Jaba trail, I see a boy and girl,

        stiff from pre-dawn rise,

Seated on a plastic tarp; mudsplattered, damp, tired, alive.

They are studying birds, holding small flycatchers

        in their hands, talking to them,

        as they weigh them before release.

I see no major Buddhas here, only a boy and girl studying birds,

        tired, breakfast in a bag,

They are admiring the rufus tints on the leaf-gleaner's tail.

A worn, pencilled, thumbed, bent, stained bird guide
              lies beside them on the tarp.
Tiny bands for tiny legs are strung on tiny wires.
Strange names in Spanish and English are used—
Names of fleet, subtle, fragile, winged and hopping lives.
From before the door of dawn, a boy and a girl were up
              in caked and muddy clothes
              to camp on the rainforest floor
              and study birds.

Maybe this is why life, profuse and opulent, exists.
Maybe all of life is only the gestation period of love.

Peru

Transformation and Interrelation

At the center of the world are sunrise, wings, a rapid running river,
        and distant mountains.
Spiraling upward from their origins everywhere, all things are in constant
        transformation, constant
        reaching out for interrelation.

At the legendary clay lick on the Tambopata River, in Amazonian Peru,
We stand with our backs to the roar of running water, descending
        from the silhouetted Andes,
And watch communities of parrots arise and wheel in complex,
        multi-organism unity.
Titter and screeching fills the air, as birds clamor for a spot on the cliff
        from which to gulp nutrient-rich clay—
Blue-headed, mealy, yellow-crowned, and white bellied parrots—
Swoop in motile clusters, depart in cacophonous solidarity.
Aggregated flocking defends soft singular lives
From tayra weasels below or roadside hawks above.

Unlike their smaller kin, macaws await their turn in mated pairs,
Patiently, diffidently, shimmering in ionic majesty—
Scarlet, red and green, blue and gold macaws:
They have stolen the spectra of the sun, smuggling light's own jewels
        inside their feathers.

Master parrots of aplomb, these long-tailed giant birds await in radiant duets,
      or threesomes,
Their solitary chick beside them, always only one,
Rare and cherished offspring of a year's uncertain outcome.
The beauty of the young is no preserve against their precarious perch
      among predators and want.
In families, not in flocks, macaws bide their time and fend.

On the highest tree above the clay-lick cliffs, a threesome of blue and golds
      attend in domesticity.
The wing of one is slung across the shoulders of its mate.
Parents interleaning shoulder to shoulder beside their chick,
Under the blessed wing they bond and preen.

Within the chaos and kaleidoscope there is a common touch:
A wing across the shoulders.
Living things reach out to bridge the gulf.

At this obscure turn on a rainforest river, amidst the internecine plethora
      of bugs and birds and buds,
Peering through the lenses of binoculars, I vicariously join the fathers and the flocks
      in their rapturous and pensive melee.
A man is no exception to the quest for interrelation.
But I will soon depart from Tambopata in the long thin motorized canoe,
As later I will slip from earth, in the same way I once arrived, new.

For this universe that brought me here, and will take me away in kind,
      I have found no explanation.
There is no belief that gives full satisfaction for the vicissitudes of time.

Here I peer at the panorama in dismay and wonder, unexpectedly remote
        and vulnerable man.
Regarding beginning and ending, I have been choiceless, and uncomprehending.

Insinuated six hours by boat beyond the almanac, and lost, I find
The same laws governing birds and rivers as the sympathies and sorrows
        that flutter on my mind:
Constant transformation, constant reaching out for interrelation,
Sunrise, a wing across the shoulders,
And distant mountains, distant mountains, distant mountains.

Hunters

Welcome to the new humanity,
Who revere the tinkling and growling panoply of life
On this vivacious virgin planet overrun by us.

Once we were all predators alive to every nuance in the rustle of a bough.
We are hunters of kinship and comprehension now.

We come from around the world to South America's tropical hinterland:
        an art teacher from Cincinnati,
        two evolutionary biologists from Oxford,
        beefy and stentorian mid-western Americans,
        and a fat European family of four
        with enough telephoto equipment to record
        and enlarge every pimple and pest in Peru's
        great basin.
Awakened at 4:30 a.m., we tramp sweaty trails of mud, festooned with
        spider webs,
To catch a glimpse of the violin-curled tip of a spider monkey's tail.
We've come to the dark and torrid Madre de Dios to use
        old neural pathways
        once designed in human minds
        for full electric chase.
Every natural image on our screen deletes accreting atrophy.

The cobalt sheen of a fleeting wing awakens a reserved and inner ecstacy.
Somewhere in our neural circuitry a glorious message flares:
You are alive—the cloaking death of safe routine is shattered.

How can we fail to delight in the saddle-back tamarin,
                mini-monkey with tiny face
                and fuzzy coat, tumbling
                tackling, wrestling with its mates
                among the leaves with abandon
                bred by lightning light agility?
Here's the red brocket deer, so confident and unaccustomed to human face,
                pushing its fusiform shape
                through thickets, its modest prongs
                pruned for forest trickery;
                shorty, rusty, plump, nonplused.
We expect of ourselves too, to pay respects to the cold immobile caiman,
                lurking resolute and unemotional
                as fate, its nefarious culinary
                strategies contextualized by us
                into ecologically appropriate
                regional cuisine.
And to the black tarantula, big as a big man's opened hand,
                and waiting where we step,
                we extend respectability
                for its environmental accountability.

The antimalarial prophylaxis, the Babylonian captivity in airplane seats,
                the midnight arrivals on thieving streets,
Are worth this reignition of our long history as ambassadors
                who carry the white flag between

the courts of life and love,

the empires of life and love.

The founders of these new access routes into the previously

impenetrable unknown,

call this enterprise: *science*.

But through the power of the non-rational, each one of us brings

along our own pain

so that we remain international

Prisoners in paradise among the hummingbirds.

Each person arrives here in the jungle from a crying corner of the crowded earth,

where he or she saw war, felt hate,

or wept into the night

over the same unstoppable abandonment

And halts: walks re-awakened in this center of communion and care,

Where every living being is a cause for pause, contemplation and rare admiration.

The effort to see, know, and understand is our mission in this embassy

to the wilderness.

Human nature is most fully fashioned at the hands of sympathetic joy

and compassion.

By loving others we discover what we need to save ourselves.

Once human beings were all predators alert to every nuance in the rustle

of a bough.

Hunters of kinship and comprehension stalk the jungle now.

India and Amazonia

India elevated our humanity, creating a culture in which
> love and compassion,
> peace and harmony,
Are the divinities we formerly personified as gods.
India, cradle land of the seated man
Who enticed us beyond identity with our bodies and our tribes
To become vehicles of universal love and peace,
Which exist invisible, immaterial, eternal,
Still among the flux of matter that we call *world*.

India was the dawn, from which rays of realization glowed,
Enlightenment effulgent among the shadows and the swords,
Revealing that every animal and pine, every man and woman,
Through the metamorphosis of time,
Are all brothers and sisters of transience, of loss,
> and of everything we find
When we relinquish grasping, and recline into the sunrise
> inside each moment.

Something endures in India's ravaged groves and congealing cities
That we can define as the only and always civilization,
The ineluctably saving wraith among the wars and psychic epidemics
> of mankind.

Now Amazonia, teach us magic!
Vast jungle zone of verdant and aqueous expanse —
You are the shaking shaman inside the uterus of life;
You, Amazonia, the drumbeat within the sap and blood
                    of fruit and fur.

Among the pungent and seminiferous odors, where the rainforest floor
                    is tramped, torn, gouged and scarred
                    by the hooves of foraging peccary bands;
Among the screams of toucans and the resonating roars of howler monkeys,
                    projecting their power and their pain
                    from hidden heights among
                    the arboreal labyrinth of limbs and leaves;
Among the queenly tropical hardwoods — kapok, brazil nut, dipteryx —
                    whose sinuous crowns tower
                    emergent and triumphant
                    above the multilayered canopy;
Among the murky, torpid, brown pools of still water
                    pestilent with caiman and electric eels,
                    demons stronger than the strongest man
                    and instant death
                    to unlucky tripped or fallen life;
Where all the molecules of planet stuff already whirl
                    in plant and animal form,
                    with nothing excess in reserve
                    but all catalyzed, activated,
                    cycling through the gates of life and death;

The endless cornucopia of the biosphere pours forth in beetles,
            ants, sloth and deer;
            capuchin, eagle, snake and boar;

Teach us, Amazonia of the humming and creaking night
            that rotates into torpid day;
Teach us of the infinitude of embryos pregnant within the foliagic curtains
            waiting to be born;
Teach us of the upward thrust and downward rot of life the indeterminate,
            of life irrepressible and turbulent,
            ignorant and magnificent;
            of life mysterious with
            suffering and release.

I have heard the rumor, Amazonia, that you still contain
            within your labial recesses
            secret and uncontacted tribes—
Humans in isolation from all others, who pursue their nurture and their truths
            in archaic and pristine
            spiritual solitude—
            private, paranoid, naked and ready to kill;
            awakened, interrelated, permeated
            with the juice of somas
            while masticating their breathing
            proteinaceous kin—
Humans in isolation and steeped in the natural ecstacy
            of unselfconscious participatory abandon
            inside the unrepentant, incestuous
            family of life.

This rumor is the truth
We, the people of Amazonia,
Wander green and growing in all the regions of the globe.
City and country, there is a part of every one of us
Never yet contacted by the civilized world.
On covert game trails winding within, the human spirit wanders,
Feet on earth, dreams feeding on soil and sun.

For me, there are two halves to every moment:
India and Amazonia, the birthless and new birth.
Inside the jungle of the heart, among the lost lovers, the desperate clinging
        to unsustainable attachments,
The uncertainty and doubts about the wisdom of our choices,
And the red heliconias of passion,
We, lost legions of humanity, wander, seeking the sweet seed of peace.
In the core of time unfolding, inside we find two halves:
Detachment, transcendence, India;
And fertility, formation, Amazonia.

Teach us the universal truths of love and peace;
Teach us magic: the parthenogenic festival
        cartwheeling from inventive leagues of life;
Teach us the birthless and new birth;

Until beyond all countries, continents and ambivalence of the heart
We transform our very consciousness and exit
Upwards and liberated from this bi-hemispheric birth.

At Home

Ācariya

Ācariya means spiritual teacher.

Teacher of self-knowledge, I bow before you.
I touch my forehead to the ground, kneeling in front of the dais
        where you sit with your wife,
        and gratitude wells up and flows
        from a source beyond my known self.
I, anti-authoritarian American skeptic; pervasive disbeliever;
        habitual discounter of facile claims
        of causality or proof; chary individualist;
        champion of the null hypothesis that
        nothing is known yet—
I bend in obeisance of trust and deference: those blossoms of the disciple's
        careful, long-tended, and deeply-rooted faith.

You have been a benevolent friend.
Not a companion, not a casual guest, you have been a source,
        a guide, a pole star.
Thousands of mornings and evenings the Vipassana meditation
        you coaxed me through
        has been my flower and my fortress.
It has transported me to the nexus where love and truth intersect
        on their beginningless cosmic journeys,
        and merge indistinguishable, commonplace, liberating.

Your discourses of intricate erudition and simple, civil concord

        have suffused me with respect and veneration,

        evoked the fullest orchestration of my finest inclinations.

Your image has hovered in my mind as the personification of love and compassion,

        those felicitous invincible graces

        that antedate and survive

        the rising and falling of world cycles.

In the meditation of loving-kindness, I have directed towards you dawn and dusk

        the efflorescence of my rapture

        and solicitude.

Without your teaching, your steady unshakable presence year after year,

        your selfless reliability,

        your multilingual transduction

        of instruction from historical era to era,

        your indefatigable travel,

        your clarifications, your refusal to

        commercialize, your jet lag,

        your overenthusiasm, your aura

        of inexhaustible concern, your long,

        long journey of care, your absolutely

        uncanny devotion to the life of strangers

        like myself of every hue and latitude,

I might still be riding quixotically among the windmills of wishes and dreams.

You never troubled me with unctious familiarity; our well-bounded

        relationship was always focused

        on meditation—its practice and its spread.

You never implied there was any culture, clothing, calling or country
        other than my own
        mundane and mercurial New England
        in which I could better manifest.
The five grains you gave us we planted and replanted on our familial soil.
Their undulant and rippling stems served us as stone and steel
        during the long noon of middle life
As we cultivated the next generation and our own harvest years.

Without you I could not have learned how pure devotion —
        free of bribe or entitlement —
        reaches out but does not attach;
        like a handwave of blessing and farewell
        between a father on the platform
        and a son upon the departing train,
        who have no point of touch
        but momentous mutuality of recognition.
Without you I would not have had daily access to the high hill
        up which I could climb
        through the seasons of my years
For renewed perspective on the great river of reality unfolding —
        perspective recurrently misplaced
        behind personal fears and mountains of paper.
Without you I could not have repeatedly meditated for a month in silence,
        well cared for among salubrious
        cottages and halls; freed from details,
And saturated by the deep tolling of India's ancient white spiritual surrender.

Without you I would not have been immersed in a community
        of diverse and various races, types, intelligences,
        skills, languages, attitudes;
        a community in which my fears and foibles
        became my offerings and my strengths,
        a community you wove around the globe
        in which I was one integrated thread.
(I once arrived in darkness, in a foreign city, on the outskirts,
        in an Arabian nights land, camels hauling freight,
        wooden wheels of heavy carts rumbling beneath desert stars;
        I was alone, exhausted, disoriented, uncertain of my
        safety or my life—greeted at the gate by a
        shouting man: "This is not a hotel—you can't come
        in here—go away and come back tomorrow if you really
        want to"—but when I spoke my name, in quiet
        voice, the gate was flung open, I was welcomed as a
        guest, as an old and cherished friend; my comfort was
        seen to—and it was you they welcomed, you
        whose door I entered, you whose teaching I carried,
        whose discipline I practiced, whose friendship I conveyed—
        it was you who cleared this path for me that safely led
        among the camels and the stars.)

You gave directions on this long and ancient road, and when I felt too frail,
        you raised the shade with which
        I'd darkened my own mind.
"Your progress on the path depends on progress you have made
        in millions upon millions of lives."
You crumbled concepts and beliefs like old brick walls
And cleared perceptions to be free of judgments and of time.

Like an iris in the eye of every thought I think, another opening
    now portends.
No static stance is anywhere, but another option always here
    also leads me on:
Direct connection to the universal, beyond.

The ācariya gives, expecting nothing in return, but pointing to the way
    of direct encounter
    he raises the blind.
Obeisance is not made to you or any man — I bow before experience of my self
    towards which you urged me on.

Now on this day, I bow before you, touching my head at the foot of your dais
    where you and your wife dwell poised
    above me where I sit
    on the long clean floor of cool stone —

All of this is in my memory now
As I meditate peacefully in Amherst, twelve thousand miles away from you,
    at home.

If There is No Heaven

October 9, 2000

If there is no heaven
Then where am I now?

Your presence in my mind today
At this time of falling yellow leaves
Pattering like imperial golden raindrops

Which mark this as the time of year
Reserved for your appearance

I am in your presence
Though you are far away

You who took my youth
Used it up
Reversed it
And gave it back to me
Depleted and doubly renewed

You who taught me how limited and bound
I might inadvertently become

And how elastic and infectious I have also been
You who learned magic languages that express
The inscrutable intimacies of speech and knowing
When shared between strangers of different colors and cloaks

You who traveled to the mountains and lakes
At the navel of the world
Where the first people once emerged from the marriage of water and sun
While the ringed mountains beamed

You who tossed back over your shoulder
A casual and insouciant voice of courage
Rising disingenuously from your receptive and vernal heart

Your occasional epistles
Randomly and unpredictably arriving
Touched again in layered confines in me
These Andes and these sonnets of the silvered heart

Amidst the purgatorial fumbling of my mundane days
You wafted me up to this high thin plateau
Where human love balances among the universal principles
Of hope, renewal, and discovery

Now I stand at the highest altar
Where even the gods cannot ascend

Only human love with its inevitable loss and demise
Can push aside all the veils and reveal
The effervescent domain

That exists only in the moment
Where there is no foundation and we cannot stand
A realization illuminates
This happy birthday on earth's eternally autumnal shores

To love without attachment
To transmit the mountain light
Is the exquisite alleviation
Under whose influence we ask:

If there is no heaven
Then where am I now?

Whatever is held in the hand or struggles to endure
Is suffering
But when someone appears newborn among the falling leaves
And strikes off alone to probe the boundaries and the continents
We all receive the pulse ·
Of the ultimately human transformation

From the broken and tumultuous cities he sees
From the observatories of the ancients
Where he gazes among star-encrusted pinnacles
From the cries in the night in the jungles where he camps

The earth rotates, the day passes,
The minds of men and women everywhere lose out
In the struggle to deduce some coherent and enduring history
From the stroboscopic episodes of our fleeting lives

And still we revel
In your pointless and beneficent traverse

If there is no heaven
Then where am I now?

Grateful acknowledgments

With special thanks to Mike:

"Streams flowing under bridges and over rocks speak every language in the world
and dictate the content of all poems."

and to Rick:

"You cannot just talk to the stars or to the silence of the night.
You have to fancy some listener, or, better yet, to know
of somebody whose mere existence stimulates you to talk
and lends wings to your thoughts...."

—Heinrich Zimmer